# Pages

MW01171588

## A Reading Journal
### for
### Young Book Lovers

## This Journal Belongs To:

_____

Age: _____

Date: _____

By Katy Sloop Roberts

Pages to Pencils: A Reading Journal for Young Book Lovers
Text Copyright © 2022 Katy Sloop Roberts

Published in the United States by Katy Sloop Roberts

ISBN 979-8-9858481-2-0

Printed in the United States of America

Book and Cover Design by Katy Sloop Roberts

Dedicated to my late dad,

# Frank Brown Sloop, Jr.,

who encouraged me to read and
record my thoughts in book reports,
incentivized by a dollar for
each full-page report I wrote,
when I was a young
lover of literature.
Thank you, Dad,

# Also by Katy Sloop Roberts

Luna and Fortuna Series:
*Mario and The Stones*
*Fortuna Finds a Family*

## Luna and Fortuna

**www.lunaandfortuna.com**

Books kids LOVE and parents TRUST

# Congratulations
## on starting your very own
## Pages to Pencils Reading Journal!

Books will take you on journeys to mythical lands, into history, and to the future. Reading will even introduce you to new friends.

From the pages of your favorite books to the words that flow out of your pencil, you are going to have fun with this journal.

Think about what you liked best in the book you read. Was there anything you did not like? What did you learn? How did the story make you feel? Would you recommend it to a friend?

Now that your thinking cap is on, you are ready to write! Grab a pencil and make your first journal entry. You will read this journal in the future and feel proud and amazed at all the reading and writing you've done!

Be creative, have fun, and happy reading,

♡ *Katy Sloop Roberts*

Author of Luna and Fortuna Books

Star Ratings: ☆☆☆☆☆

Fill in the stars with your favorite color.
1 star = a book you did not like at all
5 stars = a book you LOVE and want to read again

# Author Katy's Favorite Children's Chapter Books

*In case you need book suggestions, but not in any order of ranking because it's too hard to pick!* ☺

The Chronicles of Narnia by C.S. Lewis

The Miraculous Journey of Edward Tulane by Kate DiCamillo

Fantastic Mr. Fox by Roald Dahl

Charlotte's Web by E.B. White

Sideways Stories from Wayside School by Louis Sachar

My Father's Dragon by Ruth Stiles Gannett

Ramona Quimby, Age 8 by Beverly Cleary

Anne of Green Gables by L.M. Montgomery

Number the Stars by Lois Lowry

Fortuna Finds a Family by Katy Sloop Roberts

Mario and The Stones by Katy Sloop Roberts

# Five-Star Books
☆☆☆☆☆

*Wait to complete this page (and the next 5 pages) until you finish your journal!*

1. _____
2. _____
3. _____
4. _____
5. _____
6. _____
7. _____
8. _____
9. _____
10. _____

_____

_____

_____

# My Favorite Book

☆ ☆ ☆ ☆ ☆

*Wait to complete this page until you finish your journal.*
*Of all of the books you read, which book is your overall favorite?*
*Explain why.*

_____

_____

_____

_____

_____

_____

_____

_____

_____

_____

_____

_____

_____

_____

_____

_____

_____

# My Favorite Character

☆ ☆ ☆ ☆ ☆

*Wait to complete this page until you finish your journal.*
*Of all of the characters you met, who would you most like to have as a friend in real life?*
*Explain why.*

_____

_____

_____

_____

_____

_____

_____

_____

_____

_____

_____

_____

_____

_____

_____

_____

_____

# My Favorite Setting
## where the book takes place

*Wait to complete this page until you finish your journal.*
*Of all of the settings you visited in your imagination, where would you most like to live?*
*Explain why.*

# My Favorite Genre

types of books such as
mystery, mythology, fantasy, and biography

*Wait to complete this page until you finish your journal.*
*Of all of the categories of books you read, which genre is your favorite?*
*Explain why.*

_____

_____

_____

_____

_____

_____

_____

_____

_____

_____

_____

_____

_____

_____

_____

_____

# My Favorite Author

☆☆☆☆☆

*Wait to complete this page until you finish your journal.*
*Of all of the books you read, which author is your favorite?*
*Explain why.*

# On your marks,

# Get set,

# Write!!!

Date:_____ ☆☆☆☆☆

Title:

Author:

Illustrator:

Fiction or Nonfiction:

Characters:

Setting:

My Thoughts:

Doodle Space

Date: _____  ☆☆☆☆☆

Title:

Author:

Illustrator:

Fiction or Nonfiction:

Characters:

Setting:

My Thoughts:

Doodle Space

Date:_____ ☆☆☆☆☆

Title:

Author:

Illustrator:

Fiction or Nonfiction:

Characters:

Setting:

My Thoughts:

Doodle Space

Date:_____ ☆☆☆☆☆

Title:

Author:

Illustrator:

Fiction or Nonfiction:

Characters:

Setting:

My Thoughts:

Doodle Space

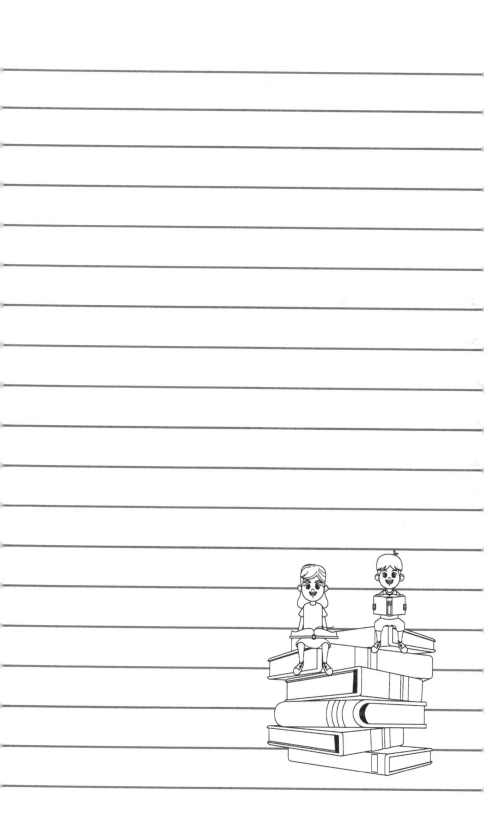

Date:_____ ☆☆☆☆☆

Title:

Author:

Illustrator:

Fiction or Nonfiction:

Characters:

Setting:

My Thoughts:

Doodle Space

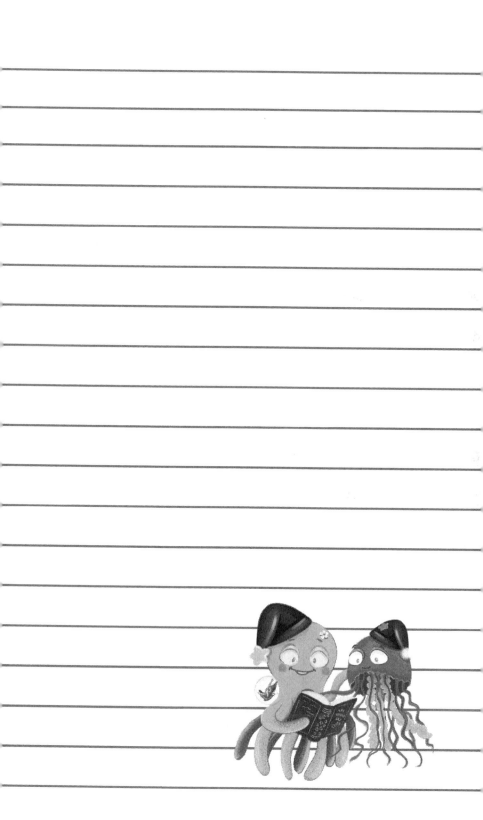

Date: _____  ☆ ☆ ☆ ☆ ☆

Title:

Author:

Illustrator:

Fiction or Nonfiction:

Characters:

Setting:

My Thoughts:

Doodle Space

Date:_____ ☆ ☆ ☆ ☆ ☆

Title:

Author:

Illustrator:

Fiction or Nonfiction:

Characters:

Setting:

My Thoughts:

Doodle Space

Date:_____  ☆☆☆☆☆

Title:

Author:

Illustrator:

Fiction or Nonfiction:

Characters:

Setting:

My Thoughts:

Doodle Space

Date:_____ ☆ ☆ ☆ ☆ ☆

Title:

Author:

Illustrator:

Fiction or Nonfiction:

Characters:

Setting:

My Thoughts:

Doodle Space

Date:_____ ☆☆☆☆☆

Title:

Author:

Illustrator:

Fiction or Nonfiction:

Characters:

Setting:

My Thoughts:

Doodle Space

Date:_____  ☆ ☆ ☆ ☆ ☆

Title:

Author:

Illustrator:

Fiction or Nonfiction:

Characters:

Setting:

My Thoughts:

Doodle Space

Date: _____   ☆ ☆ ☆ ☆ ☆

Title:

Author:

Illustrator:

Fiction or Nonfiction:

Characters:

Setting:

My Thoughts:

Doodle Space

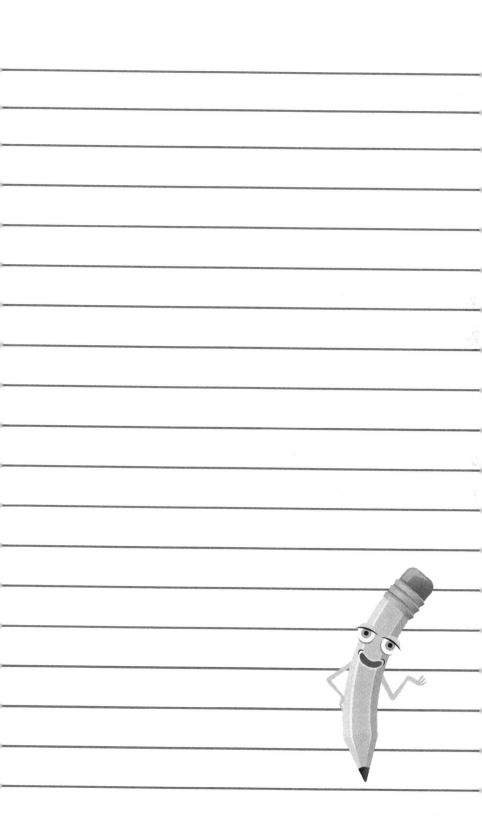

Date:_____ ☆☆☆☆☆

Title:

Author:

Illustrator:

Fiction or Nonfiction:

Characters:

Setting:

My Thoughts:

Doodle Space

Date:_____  ☆☆☆☆☆

Title:

Author:

Illustrator:

Fiction or Nonfiction:

Characters:

Setting:

My Thoughts:

Doodle Space

Date:_____ ☆☆☆☆☆

Title:

Author:

Illustrator:

Fiction or Nonfiction:

Characters:

Setting:

My Thoughts:

Doodle Space

Date: _____ ☆ ☆ ☆ ☆ ☆

Title:

Author:

Illustrator:

Fiction or Nonfiction:

Characters:

Setting:

My Thoughts:

Doodle Space

Date: _____ ☆ ☆ ☆ ☆ ☆

Title: _____

_____

Author: _____

Illustrator: _____

Fiction or Nonfiction: _____

Characters: _____

_____

Setting: _____

_____

My Thoughts: _____

_____

Doodle Space

Date:_____ ☆☆☆☆☆

Title:

Author:

Illustrator:

Fiction or Nonfiction:

Characters:

Setting:

My Thoughts:

Doodle Space

Date:_____ ☆☆☆☆☆

Title:

Author:

Illustrator:

Fiction or Nonfiction:

Characters:

Setting:

My Thoughts:

Doodle Space

Date:_____ ☆☆☆☆☆

Title:
_____

_____

Author:
_____

Illustrator:
_____

Fiction or Nonfiction:
_____

Characters:
_____

_____

Setting:
_____

_____

My Thoughts:
_____

_____

Doodle Space

Date:_____ ☆☆☆☆☆

Title:

Author:

Illustrator:

Fiction or Nonfiction:

Characters:

Setting:

My Thoughts:

Doodle Space

Date:_____ ☆☆☆☆☆

Title:

Author:

Illustrator:

Fiction or Nonfiction:

Characters:

Setting:

My Thoughts:

Doodle Space

Date:_____ ☆☆☆☆☆

Title:

Author:

Illustrator:

Fiction or Nonfiction:

Characters:

Setting:

My Thoughts:

Doodle Space

Date:_____ ☆☆☆☆☆

Title:

Author:

Illustrator:

Fiction or Nonfiction:

Characters:

Setting:

My Thoughts:

Doodle Space

Date:_____ ☆☆☆☆☆

Title:

Author:

Illustrator:

Fiction or Nonfiction:

Characters:

Setting:

My Thoughts:

Doodle Space

Date:_____  ☆☆☆☆☆

Title:

Author:

Illustrator:

Fiction or Nonfiction:

Characters:

Setting:

My Thoughts:

Doodle Space

Date:_____  ☆☆☆☆☆

Title:

Author:

Illustrator:

Fiction or Nonfiction:

Characters:

Setting:

My Thoughts:

Doodle Space

Date:_____ ☆☆☆☆☆

Title:

Author:

Illustrator:

Fiction or Nonfiction:

Characters:

Setting:

My Thoughts:

Doodle Space

Date:＿＿＿＿＿＿ ☆☆☆☆☆

Title:

Author:

Illustrator:

Fiction or Nonfiction:

Characters:

Setting:

My Thoughts:

Doodle Space

Date:_____  ☆☆☆☆☆

Title:

Author:

Illustrator:

Fiction or Nonfiction:

Characters:

Setting:

My Thoughts:

Doodle Space

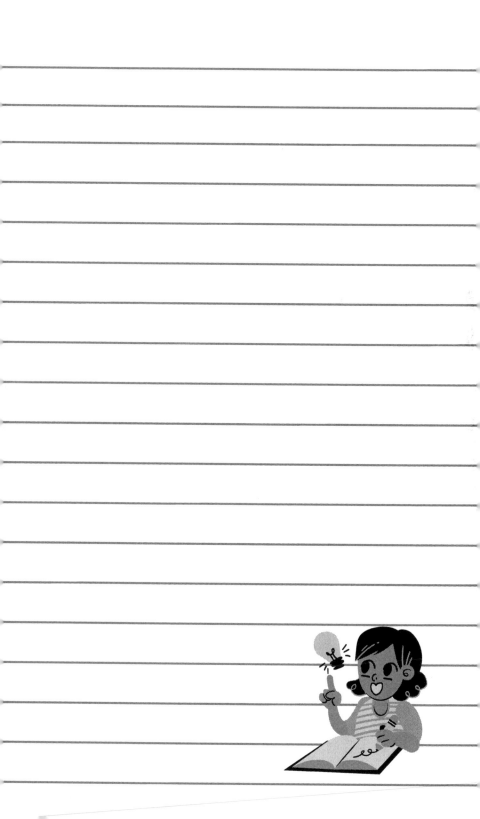

Date:_____ ☆☆☆☆☆

Title:

Author:

Illustrator:

Fiction or Nonfiction:

Characters:

Setting:

My Thoughts:

Doodle Space

Date:_____ ☆ ☆ ☆ ☆ ☆

Title:

Author:

Illustrator:

Fiction or Nonfiction:

Characters:

Setting:

My Thoughts:

Doodle Space

Date:_____  ☆☆☆☆☆

Title:

Author:

Illustrator:

Fiction or Nonfiction:

Characters:

Setting:

My Thoughts:

Doodle Space

Date:_____ ☆☆☆☆☆

Title:

Author:

Illustrator:

Fiction or Nonfiction:

Characters:

Setting:

My Thoughts:

Doodle Space

Date:_____ ☆☆☆☆☆

Title:

Author:

Illustrator:

Fiction or Nonfiction:

Characters:

Setting:

My Thoughts:

Doodle Space

Date: _____ ☆☆☆☆☆

Title:

Author:

Illustrator:

Fiction or Nonfiction:

Characters:

Setting:

My Thoughts:

Doodle Space

Date:_____  ☆☆☆☆☆

Title:
_____

_____

Author:
_____

Illustrator:
_____

Fiction or Nonfiction:
_____

Characters:
_____

_____

Setting:
_____

_____

My Thoughts:
_____

_____

Doodle Space

Date: _____ ☆☆☆☆☆

Title:

Author:

Illustrator:

Fiction or Nonfiction:

Characters:

Setting:

My Thoughts:

Doodle Space

# Congratulations!

## You filled your Pages to Pencils Reading Journal!

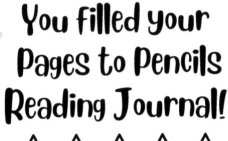

Order a new
Pages to Pencils Reading Journal
at
www.lunaandfortuna.com/shop/

**Need book suggestions?**
Look no further, get a list of 65 titles
kids love and parents trust
at bit.ly/65MGBookRecs

Happy Reading,
♡ *Katy Sloop Roberts*

Made in the USA
Columbia, SC
26 May 2024

35805839R00050